INTERMEDIATE PIANO

'Tis The Season

Arranged by
Eugénie Rocherolle

Contents

Art Design: Carmen Fortunato

© 1999 BELWIN-MILLS PUBLISHING CORP. (ASCAP)
All Rights Assigned to and Controlled by ALFRED MUSIC PUBLISHING CO., INC.
All Rights Reserved.   Printed in U.S.A.

CHRISTMAS TIME IS HERE

Words and Music by
LEE MENDELSON and VINCE GUARALDI
Arranged by EUGÉNIE ROCHEROLLE

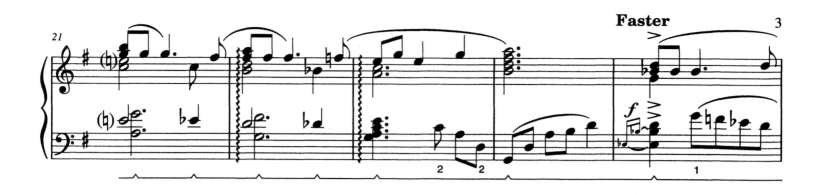

Christmas time is here, happiness and cheer.
Fun for all that children call their favorite time of year.
Snowflakes in the air, carols everywhere.
Olden times and ancient rhymes of love and dreams to share.

Sleighbells in the air, beauty everywhere.
Yuletide by the fireside and joyful memories there.

Christmas time is here, we'll be drawing near.
Oh, that we could always see such spirit through the year.

WINTER WONDERLAND

Words by DICK SMITH

Music by FELIX BERNARD
Arranged by EUGÉNIE ROCHEROLLE

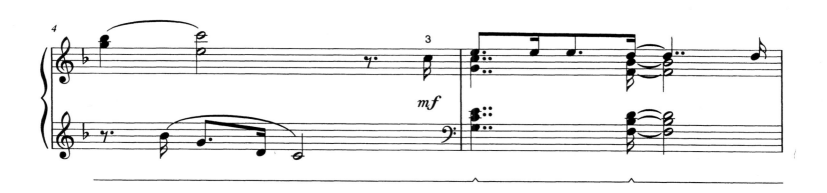

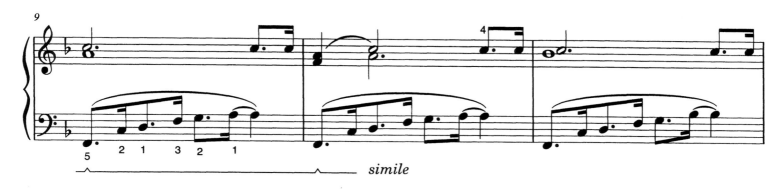

simile

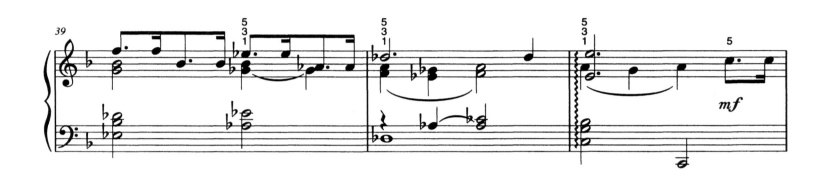

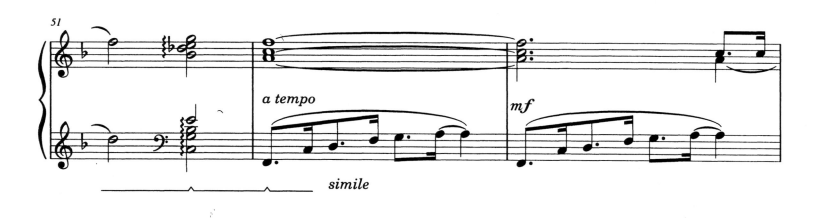

THE CHRISTMAS WALTZ

Words by SAMMY CAHN

Music by JULE STYNE
Arranged by EUGÉNIE ROCHEROLLE

WHEN BLOSSOMS FLOWERED 'MID THE SNOWS
(Venite Adoramus)

PIETRO A. YON
Arranged by EUGÉNIE ROCHEROLLE

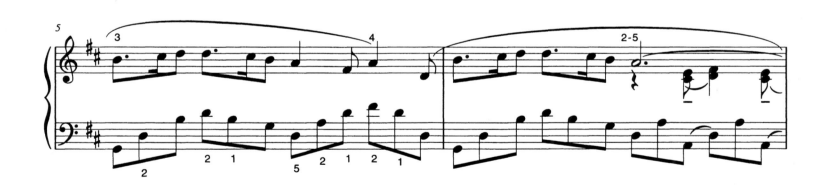

IT'S THE MOST WONDERFUL TIME OF THE YEAR

By EDDIE POLA and GEORGE WYLE
Arranged by EUGÉNIE ROCHEROLLE

Sprightly

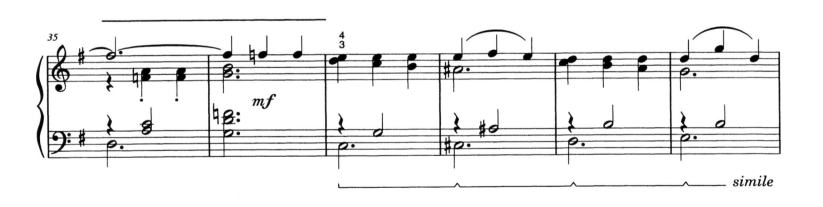

EL9921

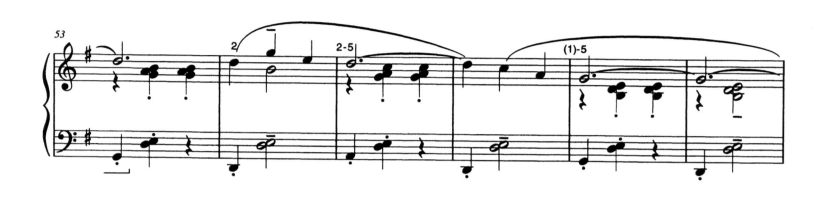

It's the most wonderful time of the year.
With the kids jingle belling, and everyone telling you,
"Be of good cheer,"
It's the most wonderful time of the year.

It's the happiest season of all.
With those holiday greetings, and gay happy meetings
When friends come to call,
It's the happiest season of all.

There'll be parties for hosting, marshmallows for toasting
And caroling out in the snow.
There'll be scary ghost stories and tales of the glories
Of Christmases long, long ago.

It's the most wonderful time of the year.
There'll be much mistletoeing and hearts will be glowing
When loved ones are near.
It's the most wonderful time of the year.

THE TWELVE DAYS OF CHRISTMAS

(Sonatina style)

OLD ENGLISH
Arranged by EUGÉNIE ROCHEROLLE

Eugénie Rocherolle

Composer, lyricist, pianist and teacher, Eugénie Rocherolle began an early publishing career in choral and band music. In 1978, with the success of her first piano solo collection, she soon established herself as one of the leading American composers of piano repertoire. Her music is widely distributed throughout the United States and abroad.

A native of New Orleans, she graduated from Newcomb College of Tulane University with a BA in music. Her junior year was spent in Paris where she had a class with the late Nadia Boulanger. She was honored as the 1995 outstanding Newcomb alumna.

A "Commissioned by Clavier" composer, she was also one of seven composer members of the National League of American Pen Women whose works were chosen to be presented in a concert at the Terrace Theater in the Kennedy Center. Awards from the Pen Women include a first place for both piano and choral in biennial national competitions.

Mrs. Rocherolle's creative output also includes unpublished works in solo voice, chorus and orchestra; musical theater; and chamber music for a variety of mediums. She is a member of the American Society of Composers, Authors and Publishers (ASCAP); Connecticut Composers Inc.; and the National Federation of Music Clubs. Her biographical profile appears in the *International Who's Who in Music, Baker's Biographical Dictionary of 20th Century Classical Musicians, International Encyclopedia of Women Composers, Who's Who of American Women* and *Who's Who in the East.*

Mrs. Rocherolle has released recordings of her piano music, *Spinning Gold* and *Romancing the Piano*, and her Christmas arrangements, *Tidings of Joy*, on an independent label, Aureus Recordings.

Mrs. Rocherolle maintains a private studio where she teaches piano and composition.